THE SECRET RELATIONSHIP BETWEEN AFRICANS AND "BLACKS"

Understanding the Conflict between Africa & it's Diaspora

TUGGSTAR TOGOBO

CONTENTS

Dedicated to the ancestors that walk with me, to everyone that laid a brick in my own development, and to the future of the African world. May we survive the turbulence.

THANKS & ACKNOWLEDGMENTS

First of all I have to thank the most high in the name my people, the Ewe's refer to this entity as, Mawu, the all in all, Allah, God. I truly believe this book falls right in line with my purpose to be a servant to the progression of my people. I believe all of the individuals and people I have encountered have prepared me for a mission I still believe I'm walking towards and I have faith these words will thrust me even closer.

I thank the alignment of the stars that ignited my genetic memory when Chuck D and Public Enemy switched on my lights and begun my journey of self-discovery, introducing me to some of the most phenomenal men and women of history.

To the children of the diaspora, African Americans and African Caribbean's, whose words, passion and desire for Africa and it's freedom led me to reconnect with my cultural lineage. The names are too many, but I am eternally indebted to you.

The teachings of Malcolm X, Martin Luther King, The Most Honorable Elijah Muhammad, Marcus Mosiah Garvey, Bob Marley, The Al-kebulan Revivalist Movement, Bernie Grant, The Nation of Islam, Dr. Kwame Nkrumah, Public Enemy, Sister Souljah, Ice Cube, Lauryn Hill, Minister Louis Farrakhan, activists in the UK, Nani Kofi, Brother Minka, Bro Leader Mbandaka, Rema, my mentors Paul Obinna and Brother Pablo Reid are just some of the names I need to hi-light. Though a special mention to my brother Trevor Hakim, who took immense time to help me through a journey of self- discovery I will be forever indebted to.

To my worldwide poetry and spoken word community, in discovering the power of the word and the ability to express, I believe it saved both my life and my sanity. It provided me an outlet to discuss my thoughts and speak words no one else was saying, and on that path I met my spoken word family, AmeN NoiR, ShakaRa and OneNess. We connected on ways that was spiritual, and demonstrated our similarities as Africans of the continent and the diaspora were stronger than our differences.

To my genetic family, whose names are too many to mention, but I have to give special recognition to my maternal Great Grand Father Togbui Adamah II, who I vehemently believe his spirit lives through me, my Paternal Grandfather, TSA Togobo. While I knew neither while living, I have begun to know in death, and wish to let the world know of their contributions in their time. To the Togobo's, Adamah's & Ga-Debeku's, my Ghanaian family, my love for you is indescribable.

My immediate family, my Mother and Father for presenting us our homeland, Ghana. Those early steps of being around our culture sewed magical seeds in me that are only now beginning to sprout. Your connection to your culture made me realize the importance of knowing, understanding and continuing this legacy.

My siblings, Michael Togobo, Mensah Togobo and Nancy Sekyi-Togobo. Having ears to listen to me rant and be an outlet of many of the things brewing inside me during the early days of my self-discovery was priceless. The ability to challenge me on information I was receiving, to seeking further queries for yourself all helped me understand myself.

To my In-laws, Godding's Daniel's & Beaton's, I literally feel spiritually connected to you all as a family. Many times around the table, I just listen, and gain further insight to the strength your ancestors had, and I see it manifest in your spirits. The symmetry of your spiritualty and strength is by no means an accident.

SPECIAL MENTION

To my beautiful wife who has made me a better person, whose spiritual strength and connection to the lineage that took her from Africa to Guyana, is truly inspiring. I thank her for her support in every way as well as the discussions, debates and the way you challenge me to be a better husband, father and man.

To my shinning light Seyna Nia Yawo Togobo. You descend from two journeys, one of the enslaved and one of the African continent. You have received strength beyond measure, an ability to walk the line and see two worlds. May you be a gift to heal and a present to build.

FOREWARD

Few things infuriate me like the hurling of insults that can go back and forth between Africans and Black people in the diaspora.

I remember watching television in England during the mid 1990's; the genesis of my Africentricism, (mainly from an American standpoint.) There was a British, Jamaican stand up comedian, Curtis Walker that did a sketch, which ripped into Africans. The auditorium of well over a thousand Black faces erupted in laughter as Africans were mocked. It was at a point where I unassumingly thought it was accepted all Black people came from Africa, thus I was gravely concerned at how backward Black Britain at this time seemed. The following day I decided to pen a letter to the leading Black figure in America, his name; Minster Louis Farrakhan. I requested him to come to Britain to spread light to the Black people who seemed to have no idea they were from Africa. (I only discovered much later he was banned.) It was a wishful letter from a naive teen that believed a speech could change everything.

As time subsided in the United Kingdom, so had the frequency of occurrences that brought the rage that I experienced while watching the comedy show. Though, I starkly remember it returning when hearing an outro on rapper Ghost Face Killer's sophomore album *Supreme Clientele*. He intimated that African girls weren't worthy of comment when discussing beauty. I never bought, nor listened to another album from him again, even though he is one of my most respected lyricists. Something about this subject gets me so riled up I have no idea where this rage comes from.

Now living in North America since 2013, the frequency of

such rage seems to be more frequent than I had grown accustomed to in the UK. I began noticing similar jabs coming from Canada and the United States as I had witnessed during my youth in England. It felt like I had travelled back in a time machine.

After one incident, I decided to post my anger on Facebook, and my thoughts drew opposition from people in North America, prompting a debating date to thrash out these issues. I was initially going to attend with guns drawn (metaphor) but instead I took time to listen. I didn't immediately respond, my head was thrown into a frenzy of thoughts, recalling the various chapters in my life for weeks after.

It was these thoughts that prompted a three-part blog on this matter, which coincided with the release of the mini-series *Book of Negroes*. The response from these blogs was so overwhelming that many people requested I compile it into a book. At the time I didn't think I had enough material. I wanted to do further research to make it an academic offering. Though, with increasing articles, and video's being promoted online that talked about the increasing tension between Africans and African-Americans, I decided that a book like this couldn't wait. During this time, I had received numerous facebook shares and postings from Dr Boyce Watkins. He was rising in prominence within the Black community in America. I listened to him, and on one of his podcasts, he just returned from Africa, telling his followers to not allow the media and ignorance prevent them from connecting with the motherland. I was immediately impressed with his character and reached out to him to support this offering. He was extremely forthcoming, so I thank him for recognizing the importance of this topic.

I don't purport this book to be an academic one; it is not full of statistics, research and cross research, surveys and conclusions. This is simply my analysis, from being a student of history, African and European. It is a collection of my experiences as someone trying to find their identity, while seeking to find answers to the ills plaguing us as African people of both the continent and the diaspora. It is a look into how Black people in Britain have navigated some of the tensions that other parts of the world are encountering and my conclusions are simply mine based upon these experiences.

Though the aim in every word is to heal our historical tensions, to find peace and understanding, cull our historical divide and more importantly find a way forward, together.

INTRODUCTION

The African diaspora is a complex multitude of different cultural groups, hailing from diverse roots through multiple paths that in the "new world," get lumped together in a box labeled Black. The expectation and indeed fear from our predominant White hosts is that these Black people identify with being one. They find strength in their oneness, and they seek to gain power from this newfound unity.

The reality however, has been anything but oneness. With each new wave of migrating African nationalities, is an addition to an already complex box of diverse Black people that look at these new migrants as anything but family. Scratch beneath the surface and you will discover a mutual suspicion in some cases, resentment in others, a distrust, bubbling on hatred that often results in a lack of empathy, preparation, a proliferation of stereotypes, prejudices and fear.

While prehistoric evidence charts that every land mass across the earth has experienced an African presence, in the more recent times, the forced migration through enslavement had Africans forcibly revisit these lands, most popularly known as United States, the Caribbean, United Kingdom, Central and South America and of course Canada.

With the ending of colonialism starting in the late 1950s, there was a new wave of African migrants that came to western countries, largely as a result of their newly formed states collapsing into chaos. They moved to the nations of their former colonial masters and Great Britain due to their aggressive imperialist campaign was an obvious destination. Britain was to be the place where continental Africans would meet their lost and found cousins, the survivors of enslavement, who were already in the process of making new homes in the United Kingdom.

These new communities upon first meeting each other didn't form strong integrated bodies. While some Africans did join the anti-racist campaigns largely fought by Caribbean's and some Caribbean's equally joined Africans in striving for independence. The average African and Caribbean lived parallel lives in Europe. Not really understanding each other, often tolerating each other, sometimes clashing in conflict or passing on generations worth of resentment to their offspring's.

England, the place of my birth hosted some of the oldest migrating African countries after colonialism. Their offspring's got the head start over other places in the diaspora in communing with our Caribbean cousins and breaking down the barriers that our parents once carried. I am one such offspring that is a by-product of a hybrid of cultures that genetically is 100% pure unadulterated African, but socially I am a complex mix of Africa, Europe and America. I am a reflection of the diaspora in a new multi-cultured integrated landscape.

One of the benefits of being a first generation is that we come from a group that can be a bridge to communicate and discuss cultural nuances at a level our immigrant parents *may* not have been able to do. And in that endeavor I feel I can relate to some of the feelings of being torn that people who are bi-racial can have. Having mixed identities. But I realized that whether its racial or national it brings forth identical feelings, with the same parallel divisions; *'I am this, I'm that, I'm both.'*

Genetically and culturally I am a part of a social group in West Africa called the Ewe people, we are spread across Eastern

Ghana, Togo and Benin. The artificial divisions placed my ancestors in present day Ghana. So I identify as being a Ghanaian born in Britain. Ironically, however my African identity wasn't born through my West African parents but born and shaped through the African diaspora community.

It was African-American and African-Caribbean's that rekindled a pride and a love for Africa that I had rarely experienced among my continental folks, but it was a love that hyper extended my love and pride in my direct African lineage.

I am someone who has developed a career in communication; I was called to stand to attention through Hip Hop, the sub-culture of an African-American experience. I immersed myself in it, to the point I believe I can think, feel and ultimately speak to the hurt and the pain of the diaspora community, but also provide a deeper understanding to the thought and actions of my genetic family, the continental African.

It is with this background that I attempt to pull back the curtain, open the can of worms, and attempt to discuss the secret relationship, the secret tensions, the open arguments, the hidden aggression that far too often consume and prevent Africans and the African diaspora (known as Blacks) engaging in meaningful dialogue. We instead throw hurtful jabs that too often exacerbates the distance. This is my lonely attempt to heal the wounds and close the gap between Africans and Blacks.

THE AFRICAN

"Till I'm laid to rest always be depressed there's no life in the west, I know the east is the best but all the propaganda they spread tongues will have to confess...." Buju Banton

For the oldest group of human beings walking the earth today; Africans en mass are astonishingly confused about who we are as a people; and the conversation gets mind bogglingly stomped starting on what do we call ourselves. The African race must be the most talked about with regards to identity in the world. You never hear an Arab regardless of generation argue of their Arabian heritage, when was the last time you heard a Caucasian discuss whether it was still relevant to acknowledge their genesis in the caucus region of the planet? Or an Asian violently say *"Don't call me Asian?"* And even as you read this you will hear ringing in your head the echoes' of familiar rebuttals coming from people of a darker hue " I'm not African!" "I'm Black, not African" or worst still "Black people ain't Africans" and "Africans ain't Black" and "Africans don't like Black people" and "Black people don't like Africans" and "Africans sold Blacks...." You confused yet?

Well to plunge even further, I was excited to watch the new African-American sit-com *Blackish*. Laurence Fishbourne declares in the first episode "We ain't Africans, we're Black. Africans don't even like us."

Trevor Hakim, a British based film lecturer advises students to watch television with what he calls an I.C.F (Independent Cultural Foundation) so you can be an active observer and not be easily influenced by the media's subversive messages. As a result, watching Black people on TV for me can be draining, (you can already see how *Blackish* had my head spinning.) however, *Blackish* for me had many elements I liked, so I persisted, even though I couldn't forget that first jab, but in my mind I believed that insult, was simply a one off. Though, during another episode the Father was looking through his son's year book to find Black associates for him. They stopped at a brother (In my opinion) from Malawi and the Father asks, "Where's that?" son replies "somewhere in Africa." He shakes his head and says, "Pass." Implication was he wasn't Black... I assume it was because he was from Africa.... (and we know no Black people are in Africa... right?) Considering America's *first* Black president is from Kenya, it rings quite ironic that this Malawi student didn't get a Black pass. So how did other continental Africans react to this series of seemingly unprovoked attack, one African friend put it this way. "I watched the first episode but it was like it was telling me to fuck off so I stopped."

Though a Caribbean sister defended this seemingly ridiculous comment. She said that she had heard Africans say that they did not consider themselves Black! "Fe real?" I thought, I mean I was aware of some of the perspectives from those that had been colonized and influenced by Arabs and the divisions that had occurred thereafter... So cool I'll give you North Africans, at a stretch maybe some East Africans... But West Africans? Central Africans? South Africans? I mean Like Black Africans? Are they not... Black?

"I'm an African, and I know what's happening..." *Dead Prez*

So in speaking with the sister, and seeing myself as an ambassador for continental Africans, I wanted to heal the divisions. I checked my emotions and did not fly into a rage that could exacerbate divisions, as I didn't feel that was her spirit, I felt, she was coming from a place of hurt. I listened to her and others discuss this topic; and the issue wasn't that we (continental Africans) didn't consider ourselves Black it was that continental Africans didn't consider ourselves the same as those in the diaspora, as one people.

I pondered, and I was pondering at the same time reading the journey of Aminata in *Book of Negros;* from a village called Bayo to South Carolina, the genesis of the diaspora, the genesis of the African in the Americas, the genesis of the Negro, the genesis of the Nigger and Nigga the genesis of Black...

It then became clear. She was right. But that rightness needed to be understood.

"Sure I'm different, but I don't dwell on those differences, I see the same in our essences..." Tuggstar

The problem with Africans and Black people, (people of African descent, which is Africans living in Africa the Caribbean, America, central and South America... people largely transported around the world via the so-called slave trade...) is that we know very little to nothing of each other, our experiences and how we have grown as Africans. And the little we do know is too often from a third party... (aka White man) So when different groups actually do meet, their perceptions of each other is charged with an electric hyper energy that quite literally explodes on first contact. It is a division like this, which results in the compartmentalizing of Black-African identity. Those born from the diaspora are Black, and those that are directly from the landmass of Africa are different, well they're African.

"AFRICANS THINK THEY'RE BETTER THAN US!"

A familiar accusation; at it's root, is not that cut and dry, it's more about the process in which events were interpreted. Let me explain. Africans recognize based on the color of their hue, that they are Black. Fact! And it is recognized that Black people are from a landmass now called Africa. But the concept of Africans being a one Black race of people is relatively new. And the contemporary Black consciousness is a response to the impact of White supremacy and domination.

It was forged at the bottom of boats when they looked around and saw different people but one color. Knowing at this extreme period of vulnerability there was a need to look beyond differences. There was a need to find ways to communicate beyond their variances. They were now dealing with something they had never in their history needed to confront, which was being oppressed solely based on the color of skin.

Genetically, Africa is the most diverse continent on earth. And at its root Africans aren't described as just Black people or African people but historic social groups that were once nations, countries or empires. Aka so-called "Tribes." When asked who they were, they would respond my people are the Yoruba's, the Ibo's, the Akan's, the Wolof, the Zulu's, etc. people they shared a common language and common experience with; Africans were as different to each other as France Germany, Ireland, Scotland and England were to each other. We had our issues with one another, they were resolved, they went to war, they had their agreements, they made alliances, they formed kingdoms, they fled they set up new homes. So when a scholarly idiot says "Africans sold themselves" creating an image of brutal heartless African mothers and fathers chasing their children around the village to sell them to any wandering White man, is a lazy interpretation of history and a distortion on reality.

THE AFRICAN & THE NEGRO

"…. We went from Nigger, to Negro, to colored to Black to Afro to African-American right back to Nigga." Talib Kweli

One of the things that no film on enslavement since *Roots* had really focused upon was the cultural exchange from newly captured African slaves to those born into slavery. Something *Book of Negroes* gave me an insight into, because for those that were captured, now in boats they scrubbed away differences to face an enemy with an agenda of returning to freedom. This was the beginning of *Black power.* This new found unity based on their color was a threat to the slave master's sovereignty, this identification had to be erased, thus enter the Negro. A new people devoid of African traits. This new Negro would look at the recently arrived African and marvel that *these Black bodies crossed the ocean. This one knows freedom, he looks like me but speaks differently 'cos he from the Freeland.'* But this new Negro was totally unfamiliar to these 'African' ways. The 'African' would say what happened to you? (Ignorant to his own uncertain future) They look like 'Africans' but don't behave in a way that is familiar to the landmass I came from, that they are telling me is a place called 'Africa.'

So now we have the emergence of the African diaspora. A people who's shared history starts outside the coastal lines of Africa. But here is the distinction, when an African is asking *who are you?* They are trying to gain an understanding of the context that drives you as a people. Your shared history, shared language, shared experience, shared traditions.

So when they look at the diaspora, the shared identity is what became the Negro experience... A new group, a separate group, a new tribe. I remember when I began to ask questions about my history, I noticed my father would use the term Negro in reference only to African-Americans.

At the time I thought that was what all Black people were called, so I asked him whether in Ghana we referred to ourselves as Negroes? He firmly said no. I understood then, they were addressing Blacks in America by referring to them in what they understood was their social group aka tribe.

In the Nation Of Islam histography, they referred to themselves as the *lost tribe of Shabazz*. And because of the inability to be able to answer these specific question about who you are, Africans too would say *you are lost*. So back to the question... Did/do the continental Africans see the diaspora Africans as Africans? What I'm saying is the continental African as a default thought process doesn't see themselves as Africans. Yes they know they are in a land mass called Africa, but the color of the skin is not what made a people in Africa.

THE NEW AFRICAN

"There is a New African in the world..." Dr. Kwame Nkrumah

A Continental African friend of mine echoed a sentiment many of us "Africans" say, that the story of enslavement never really touched them. She put it down to the fact that the experience didn't happen in her direct line so she couldn't feel it. I totally understood her perspective even if I didn't agree, nor feel the same way.

There are occasions, when descendants of the enslavement experience are speaking about this devastating legacy, that continental Africans can completely shut down. There is a total disconnect that is often interpreted as Africans having a superiority complex.

I would however choose the term pride rather than superiority, and it doesn't come from the root of "you were slaves and we were not." It is more the pride that comes from knowing one's self. As a teenager, I would attend various Pan-African centered functions (and there were very few continental Africans attending then.) I did feel a certain pride coming directly from the continent. To me it was a blessing in not having an ancestor that endured the worst experience human beings ever endured. But as a result I had an admiration and respect for the survivors. To me they were walking talking miracles and I feel if more continental Africans were aware of what happened, they too would admire the level of strength needed to endure this arduous event. However, if one has pride without the knowledge one could understand how this could be interpreted as an attitude of superiority. Though, there are so many things continental Africans feel inferior about, one thing that is known and there is a right to be proud of, is knowing one's origin. Something taken away from those that were kidnapped and made to be *slaves.*

To be honest, I even challenge the use of the term 'slave.' We dangle euphemisms around such as slave trade, or captured, or forced labor, or working for free. This puts a completely different reality in the minds of a continental African, than what these victims truly endured. I've heard continental Africans say, "hell, slavery wasn't that bad, look you have Michael Jordan now!" and they are not incorrect based on what the understanding of the aforementioned descriptions are. "Hell we had our own slavery and forced labor." (Europeans LOVE when they hear that.) This is essentially people communicating two different understandings of the same word; it's equivalent to the Butler Benson, speaking to Kunta Kinte and saying, "yeah I'm still a slave too..." If however it was consistently described as what it was... Kidnap, Physical torture and the permanent threat of torture, psychological, and spiritual abuse, (and the permanent threat of abuse) brain washing, the deconstruction of a human beings mind, body, spirit and will, humiliation, destruction of a natural family structure, pedophilic abuse, rape. These words present a much different reality in the minds of continental Africans than the term 'slave.'

Africans were not supposed to come out intact and by in large, they didn't. They came out of it with a new identity. The African was whipped out of them, they were now exclusively Negro's, Nigger's, Blacks.

Yet four hundred years later, bubbling out of a select few was a desire for a mental and cultural return to Africa. I saw and felt in them a passion that should've been killed, a strength that should've waned, an energy that was hypnotic and I took all the

African I had and drank from it. Though I couldn't feel their feelings in the same way they do, I grew to fully understand it.

What it did was give me an insight, to pick up the pieces that my forebears had left, to connect the dots and be able to find the words to communicate an understanding to my own continental folks and right back to the diaspora, something I hope this book does.

"Though for the first time in records West Indians were now meeting their infamous African cousins who only knew about each other via false information." Tuggstar

There is one person in particular responsible for igniting my life's purpose, it was the juggernauts of Public Enemy, led by the enigmatic Chuck D that ushered in a new purpose in my life. It stimulated an interest in history and the global Black condition. During the early days of finding this new path, I began writing articles, and 6 years after my initial awakening, I found myself in the same room as Chuck D, thanking him for finding me.

During the interview, we talked about a number of things, though one thing he said that has stuck till today, was that he felt that Black people in Britain were better qualified to lead the diaspora than our American counterparts. Having been inspired by Chuck D, the conscious hip hop movement, the political powerhouses of Malcolm X, Huey P Newton, spiritual guides of Minister Farrakhan, Reverend Al Sharpton, historical geniuses like Dr. John Henrik Clarke, Chancellor Williams and a number of others, I was taken aback by his analysis. I dismissed it at the time, however he believed because of the stronger connection to Africa and the Caribbean, Black Britons were able to have a better international perspective of the world.

Now that I am living in North America, I understand his assessment. England hosted the early mass immigration of Africans and Caribbean's. There is a stronger melting pot of different types of Africans in Britain that have grown side by side with descendants of the enslaved longer than any other place on earth. Some of the experiences and conversations that have happened in Britain during the 1970s and 80's are only just being had in America.

The new generation of Africans born abroad, have already seasoned and matured in the UK, while much of North America are only beginning to see the maturation of this new off-spring of African migrants.

However, if my understanding of history is correct, there are a lot of problems, schisms, clashes and mis-understandings that are about to occur.

Early in 2014, I remember being in a barber shop in Toronto and the barber of Caribbean heritage disparagingly said how "Africans irritate me, you can always tell an African" completely unbeknownst an African was sitting in the sofa awaiting his service. It reminded me of an older time in the UK. I feel the level of African and Caribbean integration today has resulted in the development of a singular African/Black British identity. Whether you are of Black African or Black Caribbean descent the Black British identity cuts through these barriers. People of direct African ancestry are increasingly influencing the culture of Black Britain. Where once our heroes were exclusively the comedian Lenny Henry, Norman Beaton, or DJ Trevor Nelson etc. today these names are added by titles such as Elba,

Oyeowolo, Okenado, Ejiofor, Boateng. Nigerians, Ghanaians, Ugandans, Kenyans... African, Black, Black-British who can speak Patua, cockney and intertwine Yoruba and Twi; who will listen to Hip-life, Reggae, Hip-hop and Afro-beat. There isn't a question about who is Black and who isn't; it would be ridiculous to claim otherwise.

The younger generations embrace their African friends and are not afraid to eat Jollof rice along with fish and chips and jerk chicken.

Rap songs may be from Black British of West Indian heritage Giggs or Nigerian Brixtonian Sneakbo, songs maybe from Zimbabwean Emelie Sande, Jamaican Omar to Nigerian Lamar, or Nigerian TY and Nigerian Tiny Temper

Whereas before, people would cockily say like I heard in that barber shop "I can spot an African a mile off" the assimilation would have some Caribbean's saying "Fe real they're African?" and some Africans equally adding "I would've thought they were Caribbean not African."

There is an extensive experience that we have had in Britain that our peers across the water are only now entering into. We in Britain have had an experience that could benefit the deeper tensions people of African descent in other countries are about to experience. It'll be jumping the gun to say that the UK is some diaspora utopia, however, I do think there is an acceptance that wherever we are going as diverse Black people, we are going to have to get there together.

DARK DAYS IN BRITAIN

Britain wasn't always the utopian hub for the unification of African people. Continental Africans particularly would hark back to the dark days and spew stories of the harassment from their Caribbean counterparts. The embarrassing Bob Geldof *Live Aid* song in 1985 (the first one) made going to school a nightmare. Africans pretending to be Caribbean's to avoid victimization, Europeanizing names (I literally had school friends that I didn't realize were Africans till much later.) and who could forget African Bum Cleaner? (A.B.C) It's an experience only privy to those continental Africans born in Britain or who experienced school in Britain.

This is not the case today. Children of African immigrants experience far less insults based on their heritage; in fact they know little of the challenges the first wave of African students went through. In many schools now, Africans are the largest minority group and their Black British and Caribbean heritage counterparts do not see this as a problem by in large. But it is a reflection of the fast paced changes that occur in the diaspora that is never communicated back to our kin in Africa, this of course creates a different psyche in individuals only one generation removed from the continent. It impacts how Africans look at other "Blacks," how they look at each other as Africans and also how they look at themselves. How much more different would this psyche be being 400 years plus removed?

THE PAY BACK

With a number of Africans and Caribbean's mixing in Britain from the 1970s-1990 there was a level of heightened consciousness that was seeping into the mainstream, propagated by both

Rastafarians, and Black America.

During the struggle for British equality, activists were looking towards America for guidance, and they used direct tactics from the United States civil rights struggle as the first bus boycott in Bristol, England demonstrates. Though there was also the influence of Black power philosophy, which synchronized with Rastafarianism thought, consequently several offshoots to American organizations begun to emerge, like the Black Panthers. Malcolm X's brief visit to the United Kingdom gave birth to Michael X. The point being conscious, political and Africentric thought was seeping into the homes of the new Black British class of Caribbean descent. As the children began to grow there was a healthier respect for Africa and it's history, and the connection that Caribbean's had to Africa; this was expedited by the broadcast of Alex Haley's *Roots*. For the first time in some people's world, they begun to see the direct connection the diaspora had to Africa. It explained many of the thoughts broadcast on Reggae music, but not fully comprehended. This was by no means unanimous, but the idea that Africa belonged to *"us"* as Black people of Caribbean descent begun to be a rising phenomenon in Britain. Consequently, organizations echoing this transition begun to emerge; Pan-African groups like the Pan African Congress Movement, All African People's Revolutionary Party, Al-kebulan revivalist movement, were all organizations led by Black people from the Caribbean.

On the other hand, you now had a growing population of Africans that were born in the United Kingdom. They had a stronger character and sense of self-identity as Africans born in Britain. They grew up remembering harassment they got for being African. And unlike the meeker African parent or newly arrived

African immigrant, or the sole African outnumbered on the school playground. They were not standing for harassment and insults. They would fight back, they wouldn't sit at comedy shows and embarrassingly smile as the Caribbean comic ripped into Africans.

They spoke back with the memory of being victimized. This may have been through arts, through song, comedy or sometimes, physical confrontation. Insults of being an ABC, was returned by Caribbean's being labeled "Jamo's" and some of the growing conscious Blacks would speak of the victimization they received from Africans.

Some Africans would even use the disparaging comment of slavery dismissively saying "well we sold you all anyway..." This of course brought further antagonism. With Caribbean Blacks feeling enraged by being reminded of the hand Africans played in the sale of their ancestors.

Such conflict would always pain my soul, for it was a reflection of our mis-education that was being fuelled by hurt, though it seemed everyone wanted to stand like warriors and fight to the death, and no one wanted to truly understand each other's true history for the benefit of our Black British community.

AFRICANS AND THE SLAVE TRADE- "The paralysis of analysis"

Most "Black" people, be it African or diaspora, do not submit or even believe in an African centered form of education, so much of what we know about each other comes from the Euro-centric perspective of who we are, which is received without the deciphering of natural bias that would be contained through a European lens. Many parents do not know the specifics of what is taught in Eurocentric curriculums and the damaging effects on the psyche this has. So having worked in the public school system in the United Kingdom, (which I don't think is too different from anywhere else in the English speaking diaspora) let me explain what is taught in schools to our African and African-Caribbean children when it come to the enslavement period.

"Let me make it clear, Europeans did not invent the slave trade as Africans were already selling themselves, Europe merely created a new market for Africans... But it was the British that abolished it."

That statement doesn't speak to any of the reality. It speaks as though Africans weren't also victims. A brilliant segment in the **Book of Negroes**, is that it spoke of the frustration tribes felt about being constantly harassed and raided, the loss of man power, the inability to oppose the raids. In reality it fuelled deeper resentments and conflicts among groups in Africa. Even though today Africans say, "hell my ancestors weren't slaves." It is not acknowledging that a brother, uncle, cousin, auntie, niece to one of their ancestors could have been. This is why an African centered perspective is so important, because this dismissal fails to look into the actual experience from a continental Africans' point of view as being more than just a collaborator with the Europeans. For if you look into an African perspective, there is another version of events, which is seldom focused upon.

Below are just a few remnants of history evidenced through song and writing.

My maternal family descends from a royal lineage, an area named Somé in present day Ghana. My mother discovered some ancient artifacts from the late 1800's and donated these findings to the BCA- Black Cultural Archives, (which is the first institution that documents the presence of Black people in Europe.) One of the documents found was written journals scribed by my great grandfather. He learnt English and for some reason began documenting (also in English) the oral stories that were passed down. One of which alludes to the beginning encounters of Europeans and enslavement.

1) A large segment of the Ewe population of present day Ghana is a coastal group, so Ewe's would have had direct contact with this event called slavery. One story my great grandfather scribed was from a mid 16th century event. He spoke of how Europeans poisoned their water storage containers with alcohol. He said a few people consequently passed out and they were snatched and taken to Europe, but returned 3 years later speaking like Europeans and they were involved in taking more people to Europe. Who were these people? Collaborators?

2) There is an Ewe festival celebrated every year named Hogbetsotso. It celebrates the migration of the Ewe people from the Kingdom of Notsie, to present day Ghana. The Ewe community in Britain decided to continue this tradition. There was a popular song that I loved the rhythm of. I had no idea what was being said, but because the song was so hypnotic, I asked my mother to translate the words, she said, "the white man came

and asked some of us to dance on their boats and they went and they never came back."

3) I remember meeting a man from the Fra Fra "tribe" (in northern Ghana) he had two tribal marks on either cheek. I conveyed to him that I had been familiar with one scar on the cheek of the Ashanti people, but not two. He said 'before White people used to steal us. We had one scar on our cheek at the time, but we got wise to their activity and they found it difficult to continue. So as a result they started using the neighboring tribe who had one scar on their face. This shocked us because we considered them brothers. But for whatever reason they began collaborating with the Europeans, so our chief gave an order for us to use 2 marks on our cheeks and whenever a person without two marks was seen they were to be killed on sight.'

These three separate recollections tell the beginning encounters Africans had with the period of enslavement, which is a vastly different perspective from that which is taught in Eurocentric classrooms.

Black British historian Robin walker who has extensively researched the enslavement period says that when you look at the evidence, enslavement happened in different phases. The first phase was Europeans snatching people directly; but as people began to be more suspicious they adapted their approach by being more cunning and establishing partnerships with particular groups. The above stories seem to confirm this.

Now for *"Black"* people in the diaspora, I want you to see this period from the perspective of a continental African. Because from an African's perspective this side of the story is all they knew. "Some of our people were snatched by the white man. Or snatched by another group and taken to the Whiteman and we never saw them again." THATS IT!

The knowledge goes no further. The memories of these individuals would be remembered and mourned by their immediate family, stories told to succeeding generations and eventually forgotten. Thus the dungeons, the middle passage, the breaking of the African, the creation of the Negro, the Nigger, the rape, torture, the abuse, the breaking of families, the shame, the taking of names, changing of religions, enforced acceptance of Christianity, the brutality, the whips, the lynching's, the hanging, burnings etc. was completely unknown to those that remained in Africa.

So let's move forward 400 years. The early 1960s, Ghana has gained its independence. It sends its newly independent citizens abroad. Other African countries in preparation for independence also send numerous students to predominantly European universities. My grandfather was part of Ghana's first administration and worked in the Ghanaian embassy in Britain. This mass enrolment of African students in British universities comes a little after Britain invites citizens from the Caribbean to come to the UK to help rebuild Britain after the devastating Second World War. They had been in the UK for roughly ten years before continental Africans began arriving as permanent residents. My grandfather said he saw these Caribbean's and because they were Black assumed them to be Africans, but he was surprised when he interacted with them and got nothing but hostility. Only after he undertook some research did he understand who they were. The offspring's of those that were taken.

It must be understood, this journey is not something

extensively studied in African schools either. Africa's own educational practices were interrupted by a colonial education that is still by in large in place. Black people in the diaspora often forget or are not aware of how the African psyche was re-aligned during colonialism, and because this realignment happened on African soil, much of what was lost is not acknowledged, or accepted by the continental African, for often times their encounter with Europeans has been disguised as progress. This lack of knowledge can also give rise to another potentially explosive clash with the born again African in the diaspora.

"I wasn't born in Ghana, but Africa's my mama..." Dead Prez

It is not uncommon in the diaspora to meet 'born again Africans,' the Black man or woman that has immersed themselves in everything African. They have taken back African names, feel comfortable in African garments and have awaited their whole life for the pilgrimage back to the motherland. They return to Elmina Castle with tears streaming down their face and meet Africans completely desensitized to their reality and dismiss this "silly" reaction wondering, "Why are you crying? You are from the great America... or Jamaica" And the descendent now feels completely embarrassed for holding on to that piece of African culture s/he feels foolish for clinging on to, the new conclusion. "We ain't Africans ya'll. We're Black! Africans don't even like us!"

Thus there is often a certain naivety continental Africans exhibit when first entering the diaspora. Much of what has got into our minds about Black people in the diaspora has been hammered in by the media, both stating the glorious riches that are available and also the horrific acts of violence that occur in Black neighborhoods.

Of course new immigrants do not want any part of the gang violence, high drop out rates, prison and street crime that are identified as being Black American, neither do they want to be a part of the street organizing, militant and activist culture that seemingly blame everything on White America.

As immigrants, they want to identify with their national communities, make it in the mainstream and grasp the apparent opportunities that didn't exist for them in Africa. Above all, however, they wish to mount a challenge to achieve that 6-figure salary, big house and send some money to help their family members back home.

Therefore, the reality of police brutality, discrimination is seen as part of the dysfunctionality of Black American culture and therefore it would be best to distance themselves from that. However, they are largely unaware and often unconcerned with how things got so bad in these Black communities.

The same happened in Britain during the 50/60s. Continental Africans didn't communicate much with the Caribbean's that received the sharper edge of racism, who began having children a generation before Africans migrated en mass, whose children were demonized in school, put in classes for low ability, whose parents were hard working and as a result hardly home, whose children were more so on the streets receiving the attention of police officers. Who would make the news as mischief making, criminals, and gangster's known for smoking weed at carnival, which every year would descend into violence.

What did our African parents, often university graduates, business people, former government minsters think of these West Indians? 'Stay away from them! They are trouble.' But what happened when the next wave of Africans arrived, economic refugee's, that sought any job and any residence, whose neighbors were now Caribbean's, whose children went to the same schools, suffered same challenges, all of a sudden the news reports are not only about Jermaine and Leroy, but Kofi, Ade and Ola. African parents one to two generations deep began to ask, what is happening to our children? Caribbean elders would say, "Exactly what happened to ours? Y'all became Black!" The destiny will be no less different on American shores.

THE CHANGING AFRICAN

With this change, there is a changing in understanding in our people in Africa of what it means to be an African. And the first generation of Africans born in the diaspora is the testimony to that.

On first appearance I, as a first generation African can be deemed just as *"lost"* as any other Black person. I do not have a full command of any other language accept English and not being fully versed in the ways of my people, or not knowing the language I feel that distance. Though not a distance the Black diaspora feels, for it is at least a distance I can touch if not grasp; our walk, our talk our sensibilities maybe that of the diaspora... Once thought of as "White," so sure, some people would look at me and label me "the White man." not because of my skin color, but because my life span has been spent outside. Africans do not judge on color but on context. So when Blacks of the diaspora return to African countries like Ghana and they are told they are abronnie (White) the African on the continent has no idea this is as close to the biggest insult you could ever give, but it's not meant in a derogatory way; it's about Africans understanding your context and from what they know, your context is from that of the Whiteman's land, i.e. White! This is fuelled further by when their brother, cousin, nephew, niece etc. returns home after spending a few years abroad, boasting on how they are no longer African, but English/German/American etc.

But there is a distinction between the first generation African and those of the diaspora, and it is an important one. When they ask me for a name and it is given it says TOGOBO.

They may now raise an eyebrow and ask where did I get that name? "My father is from Anloga. I'm an Ewe, from the Volta."

In some cases the response would be, "oh from the house of Togobo... Oh your father got a scholarship and went abroad. Oh you grandfather is the Great so and so. Oh well you are home then."

The distinction is they can now add a context and connect the dots to my story, which can wash away the stench of "Whiteness". Would the same conversation happen with descendants? It may. When Muhammad Ali returned he was able to explain his context to the point he was seen as an "African brother" which is powerfully documented in the documentary "When we were Kings" and I have heard more than enough similar reports with Black people from the diaspora with similar cultural leanings.

AFRICA'S DEBT TO THE AFRICAN DIASPORA

"Africa for the Africans, for those at home and those abroad"
Marcus Mosiah Garvey

It may come as a surprise to many continental Africans the level of admiration that Pan African organizations had (have) towards Africa.

I remember being at events and drawing a parallel to the African continent being seen in much the same way as Christians would idolize heaven; from songs slogans and affirmations about the great African continent, and it being the embodiment of freedom.

As Africans arrived as property, the new Negro would marvel at this guy that looked like them with a major distinction. They were once free. Having enjoyed freedom, the African would reminisce on the beautiful days before capture, and growing in the minds of some slaves, was the idea that only Africa could bring us freedom. The beginning seeds of pan-Africanism, "Africa for the Africans, for those at home and those abroad."

It is no wonder in this climate; Marcus Garvey's *Back to Africa* campaign was so popular. And in an added hint of irony, it was this pan African movement forged abroad that would inspire Africans on the continent.

And this is the clash. Perspective. Where Africans abroad, see the need for Africa to unite as a no-brainer, theories (and often impractical theories) are erected. 'Arabs need to leave, we should do away with Islam and Christianity, Swahili is the most commonly spoken language so it needs to be the single language in Africa. We should do away with national borders and be one people.' In principle, there is merit in many of these perspectives.

But on the ground, the continental African sees such things as completely ludicrous.

It's difficult to persuade a Yoruba who rarely comes across a Swahili speaker to pick up the language. To tell a Gambian Muslim or Ghanaian Christian to ditch these religions and for Arabs to return to Saudi Arabia in real terms just isn't a realistic proposition on the continent, it is as impractical as large amounts of Blacks in the diaspora returning to their ancestral home. Even when you go to continental Africans in the diaspora, their main focus is on how to develop their small pocket of a region in a country that has been neglected for years. And even on African unity, many groups are still debating the best method for communicating with their so-called tribes that are across 2 or 3 countries. And some of their conclusions present more problems, i.e. breaking away from the colonial established countries and re-form a nation with their historical "tribal" kin. The pressing issues for those in Africa are often different than those outside.

This is not to say there isn't any merit in the diaspora analysis. But this clash of perspectives was a sticking point for even Ghana's first president, Kwame Nkrumah, for as he was preaching the need for African unity, presidents of other countries said, "we are just focusing on our newly independent countries right now." People in Ghana grew frustrated at his frequent international visits and thought he was neglecting pertinent issues back home. But Dr. Nkrumah, like many Black Americans understood something that continental Africans didn't always grasp, which is the greater threat of White supremacy and it's impact on African sovereignty; and how did Nkrumah know? It was from his experience in the diaspora.

NKRUMAH ABROAD

Dr. Kwame Nkrumah was voted by the continent as being the man of the 20th century. He beat the favorite Nelson Mandela to the post. And considering Mandela's greatest achievement happened a few years before the end of the century and Nkrumah's occurred in the 1950s, it speaks to how highly Nkrumah was thought of from the entire African continent.

Dr. Nkrumah really understood the plight of the African diaspora. He studied in New York, before going to London, England and while in America he took time to study and to get to know the Black American.

He joined the Harlem writers group with esteemed Black people like Dr. John Henrik Clarke and Langston Hughes. He got to experience the strong arm of racism and to critically think about how to reverse the effects of slavery and colonialism; how to free Africa and how to connect with the African diaspora. His hero was Marcus Garvey, and while Garvey was the Father of Pan-Africanism, succeeded by W.E.B Dubois, it was Nkrumah that would be charged with implementing the vision for a united Africa, and he did that because he knew there was a window, that if African countries weren't organized it would be vulnerable to what he termed neo-colonialism, something we all now know far too well.

That's why Ghana's failure as the first Pan-African country in the world was so devastating. He formed a government that invited progressive Pan Africans from the diaspora to participate in its construction. People he had learnt the promise of the African dream, and the need for a united Africa from. People like George Padmore from Trinidad, Maya Angelou and John Henrik

Clark from America, he invited W.E.B Dubois to write the African encyclopedia (he eventually died in Ghana) and even when Malcolm X was entering his last days, Nkrumah invited him to stay safe in Ghana. (Imagine that) Although X didn't take him up on his offer, he was inspired to start up the *Organization of Afro-American Unity*, which was the American wing of the *Organization of African Unity.* (Pre African Union.)

Even though the state failed, powerful seeds were sown and the effects are still seen today. When we speak about the relationship between Africa and it's diaspora, there is no country in Africa that receives descendants of Africans like Ghana.

During the 1990's there was a further exploration of this relationship, with the establishment of Pan African events such as PANAFEST and Emancipation day.

There was the African & African-American summit that happened on the shores of Ghana. Former President J.J Rawlings invited the Nation of Islam to host their first Saviors day convention outside the United States under the banner *Re-uniting the African family.* There was a concert where invited artists from the diaspora like Public Enemy, Stevie Wonder and Jermaine Jackson among others returned home embraced in splendor for this occasion.

It was during this time that a young artist named Reggie Rockstone, influenced by Public Enemy, noticed that young people were trying to copy American artist, so he founded a new form of music that combined traditional Ghanaian Hi-life with the African-American sound of Hip Hop and called it "Hip-Life" ushering a new type of artist rapping in their traditional tongue, a tradition continued through to today.

"THE WHITE MAN IS THE DEVIL...." *To the Diaspora....*

"The White man is *the* Devil!" Extremely strong words, arguably the strongest words ever said to White people in response to racism. Probably the only term that could be put on the same plato as Nigger! (Perhaps) And while, I know this is a gross generalization and many in the diaspora do not subscribe to this belief and attitude at all, it *is* a term that did originate in the diaspora, and had many individuals, groups and organizations fall into this line of thought. It is a linguistic reflection of the historical realities of a group of people that begun to respond to racism through the use of extremely strong language. It is only something that could have come from the 20th century Black diaspora.

I have often heard it being said that had Barack Obama been a *Black* American, he wouldn't have gotten elected. Farrakhan said that the kernel of attitude in children of the enslaved isn't present in Africans. (Except maybe our southern African brethren's for obvious reasons) Who knows? But one thing is likely, there would've been some relative of an African-American candidate that was a former (or current) "Black radical" and he would have had to justify his position to this perspective, however, with Obama's Black relatives in Kenya, he could side step this potential minefield a lot easier, though he still needed to survive the litmus test and position himself in relationship to the Black activist traditions. Both Minister Farrakhan and Reverend Wright were put in front of him as stumbling blocks, but with no direct history of activism or experience that could rival that of Black America, his election was seen as a lot safer to White America than say an individual like Jesse Jackson.

If you were to ask the earlier group of Africans that encountered White people, they would've probably stood side by side with the 20th century Black diaspora. Many historical African figures that resisted slavery and colonialism had little trust or affection for the European "invader" giving them names, which at the root would today be seen as offensive.

However, the 20th century continental African generally doesn't appreciate the source of Black rage. Equally the Black person in the diaspora couldn't understand after all Africa had suffered at the hands of White people, why they weren't as angry and suspicious of them as they are. I remember witnessing these different attitudes clash in the activist community in London and to be honest both views are completely justified and understandable, but the dance can be a tricky one to master.

Continental Africans are often amazed listening to the radical preachers that picked up the baton after Malcolm X departed. They often can't believe people could talk as bold about the wrongs done by White people. They would often say their analysis is both unfair and racist, especially when they do not know the historical context to their anger. It is critical to understand Malcolm X's and the like's venom and fierceness as individuals that represent an emotionally genetic charge of ancestral spirits that were muzzled. That lived and died with no other experience than racism and servitude. Tupac Shakur once said "we aren't even rapping, we are letting our dead homies tell stories through us." Understanding that, it was inevitable a voice like Malcolm would manifest, and speak for those that couldn't and for those too afraid to. When it did appear, there was a collective cheer, for Black people in the diaspora had never seen a man like him that could speak their thoughts and frustrations so fearlessly. With many injustices today rooted in the treatment of yesteryear these voices are still often celebrated by a Black community that crave a power they are yet to see.

It must also be understood by the Black diaspora that the White man that colonized Africans grew to know (with the exception of South Africa) was radically different than the White man governing Black people in "the new world."

The continental Africans' resistance to colonialism was subdued by a variety of violence, bribery, befriending and brainwashing techniques.

By the end of the colonial era traditional forms of worship were taboo and they were now in admiration and awe of the very people they were a century before trying to keep off their land. They had been totally conquered physically, emotionally and spiritually. The people who had once governed with sophisticated political and spiritual systems around their so-called "tribal identities" like Yoruba, Ibo and Ashanti's etc. were now simply Christians that believed their ancient beliefs were of the devil. Though, what was even more stark, was because they were still in Africa, surrounded by Africans, they by in large had no idea to what extent this colonial educational system had penetrated their psyche and effected their sense of who they were. Thus by the time the struggle for independence had been won, their ability to govern the land they once did in most cases failed miserably. They couldn't see people of differing social groups as family. It quickly descended into civil chaos, civil mis-management, conflict for power and in some cases genocide. Africans, saw their African brothers and sisters rule with complete disdain and disregard for human life. Many activists' were saved from the brink of death by well meaning White journalists, politicians, individuals, organizations and countries; it was near impossible to look at this White man or woman in the face and see evil, when it was this

White man who granted them political asylum, who provided a safe house, gave their family a safe environment to live in. The Conclusion was therefore "the devil lies within, whether Black or White. Though he is more likely to be Black. And if I still fight for justice, it would be based on the rule of law, not the color of skin." The conclusion of those in the diaspora however, is that every wicked act can be traced back to that of the White man!

Most continental Africans, given the choice would sooner embrace the doctrine of Martin Luther King than Malcolm X. This in large part may be due to the religious connection for many, but it is also the belief that the strategy of love speaks to the nature of how Africans like to co-operate with people who are not African.

Martin Luther King was able to tap into this spirit of African people, and be an example to all other racial groups that regardless of the treatment you have received past or present, we as humans can rise above our differences and live happily in a co-existence. An olive branch that the descendants of Africans held out to their former oppressors and enabled to create a once unimaginable relationship between people who should've been eternal enemies.

THE LESSONS FROM ENSLAVEMENT

"Know for certain that your descendants will be strangers in a land that is not theirs, where they will be enslaved and oppressed for four hundred years. "But I will also judge the nation whom they will serve, and afterward they will come out with great substance ..." Genesis 15:13-16

It is believed by many that during the enslavement period God had abandoned Black people. Many people point to the story in the bible of the descendants of Abraham being enslaved for 400 years, and believe this prophecy was not of the historical Jews in Egypt, as no historical record speaks to that event, but it was a passage prophesizing the impending enslavement of Africans.

I've sat in many conversations where descendants of those kidnapped discuss and dissect this period from a political, spiritual and historical perspective in an attempt to draw meaning and significance from their holocaust. "Was it their strength? Their weakness? Was it karma? Were they being prepared for something else? Is there still a lesson to be learned?"

"How Many Leaders you said we needed then left them for dead?" Kendrick Lamar

It suddenly dawned upon me, that what if it was a lesson that we are yet to learn? With little respite during the 400 year enslavement, I can easily see how God seemed to abandon his flock. I can't say this exists at the end of enslavement. From a spiritual and political perspective, God has raised and sent some of the greatest leaders ever given to human beings to people of African descent. The list of names that have come to Black people

46

has been endless. What if the problem is not in the messengers, but the people they've come to save?

I've heard the perspective that unifying based on racial identity for people of African origin has not been successful. And I agree. I agree that we more successfully unify around culture, we unify around beliefs, around religion, around political ideas, but not on race. We've tried, but it hasn't succeeded. BUT! What if that was the lesson? What if that is the task that we must still learn?

As people of African descent throughout the world, we have done an absolute world class, and admirable job in being able to forgive, empathize and see the humanity of different racial groups especially White people. We have mastered putting their concerns and feelings above and beyond ours. But on the same card we have done a pitiful job in extending that same honor to ourselves as people of African descent. We have seen the humanity in others, but not the God in ourselves.

There are many bad things that have happened to us and are still happening to us that will cease to happen over night if we did something as little as see the God in us. As silly as it may sound and as ambitious as it may be, I ask, was that the lesson?

The progress Africans have made in racial equality is undeniable. That when Africans were shackled at the bottom of boats, just the mere thought, or suggestion that one day one of their descendants would be able to love individuals of white skin would've been preposterous, that a whole movement based upon seeking a co-existence with the same man or woman would have been unthinkable. But look where we are now?

How far would that whole industry of enslavement have

gotten if there was a thinking that this is family and we are not getting involved in doing business with the White man, or the Arab over our brother or sister of the darker hue. It may have resulted in a war; a defeat may have just delayed the inevitable. But a victory would have created a completely different universe.

THE MARCH FORWARD

Are we in need of new ideas, think tanks to erect a new strategy moving forward for African people, continental and diaspora Black? As cliché as it sounds, the first step needs to be a deeper education to understand ourselves, our journey, our nuances, our differences, so we can better reach our similarities.

The need for African people to go through an Afri-centric educational process in all areas of pursuit is not only a basic need, but also essential for our integration as a people. It has the power to diffuse conflicts among us that have been left to fester, it has the power to inspire and empower our pursuits, add context to where we are, how we got here and what we must do. It enables us to empathize, get to know each other as people of African descent, from one root, to its many branches. How else will we get to know each other if we are not actively attempting to learn about each other?

Africans and Blacks both in the diaspora and the continent have got to know White people very well because we have been immersed in their educational systems. Africans and Blacks both in the continent and diaspora can read this text with White lens, and know instinctively which word, which line, which phrase may be seen as offensive to them. We feel it within our own Black bodies. Though at the same time, some of the points made in this very book about our fellow Africans and Blacks maybe thoughts we are considering for the first time, ever! This is how far away we are from thinking within our own African framework. Africans that have been Arabized, are equally adept at understanding the Arabian mindset, being in tune with their educational doctrine and are equally as distant in empathizing with the diverse African experience.

This is, however not saying attempts to integrate our experiences hasn't been done before; I would suggest positive steps have been taken during the African resurgence in the 20th century, with astounding results. For example,

1) The lowest rate of gang activity and drug activity in deprived areas in America was when the Black panthers were highly active in the United States. They provided breakfast clubs and after school programs for their community. They had an international view of the world, and were seen as heroes by the local community.

2) U.N.I.A and the Nation of Islam under Elijah Muhammad both created jobs, home improvement and economic prosperity, The Nation of Islam took Garvey's efforts a step further and had erected a multi-million dollar economy which started from a school, that went on to include businesses like dry cleaning, laundry, restaurants to farmland, a printing house, housing complex's and a hospital. Both doctrines had a strong focus on boosting one's self esteem, increasing their confidence and loving, respecting and getting to understand the various experiences of people of African descent.

3) In Africa, Kwame Nkrumah was very aware of the impact of colonialism and the ticking time bomb of tribalism. He ensured education was free and people of different social groups were

forced to be educated together, sharing dormitories, sharing languages, culture, customs and ideas. This act alone defused the potential for rifts early on and while countries to the left and right imploded along tribal lines Ghana's didn't.

4) Thomas Sankara eradicated Burkina Faso's dependency on foreign aid and increased productivity of its own economy in just 4 years. Producing its own products, creating new economies, all because of the look inward at their own abilities.

Though, when one researches into why much of the above eventually failed, you will find many different answers from outside manipulation, infighting, corruption etc., but at its root, the inability of Black people to see each other as true family enabled outsiders the power to manipulate differences and ultimately control the outcome of their demise.

Today, from Chicago to Kingston, Stonebridge in London to Haiti and The Congo, the biggest problem of African people throughout the world is seeing the God in us as Africans of the darker hue?

Far too often the answer to "where are you from?" is met with an attitude that could range from anger, mistrust to straight murder.

If any other group eradicated itself on the level people of African descent are doing, it would be considered genocide and declared a state of emergency. Our current level of apathy is unacceptable and our existence requires a complete overhaul, from the root to the fruit, our future and place throughout the world depend on it.

My final belief is that we must be as serious at African

integration as we have been with integrating with White people. We don't only know the psychology of White people we are their conscience and can defend their concerns better than our own. What if we began the footsteps to integrate ourselves in that way? To understand each other as people from the African continent and Africans in the diaspora. Right to the point we know what offends other Africans, we know how different Africans got to be different Africans. What if for the first group of people to walk the planet earth, our lesson is to now treat each other as if we came from the same essence, the same continent, the same God, and to find ways to love the diverse African hue's we have been blessed to be clothed in?

What if the lesson we need to learn is that our differences are opportunities to learn not scorn? And as a people our aim is to decide on a direction and agree that wherever we decide to go, we go there as a diverse group of African people, but together!

Tuggstar Togobo

ABOUT THE AUTHOR

Andrew 'Tuggstar' Togobo is a graduate of History and International Politics (BA hons) at Coventry University in the United Kingdom. After graduating, he went on to publish numerous articles as a freelance journalist in both *Untold & New African magazine, eventually* becoming a regular columnist for British Black newspaper *New Nation*.

In 2001 he moved to Toronto, Canada for a year, it was there he began to take performance poetry seriously. He arrived back in the UK as an internationally respected poet. After 15 years of doing poetry, he has performed alongside the likes of Dead Prez, Estelle, Amiri Baraka and Linton Kwesi Johnson. He has featured on British Hip hop legends Blak Twang L.P. **Speaking from Experience;** And opened for former president of Ghana J.J Rawlings.

He has been interviewed on numerous media outlets including the BBC, Time Out Magazine, and numerous radio stations across the UK, America, Canada and Ghana.

He has published a chapbook called **The Way of the Word** and to date has two albums **The Africa E.P From Here to There and Home Again** and **Season of Lost Love.** He is currently working on his third *album* **Family Ties.**

Tuggstar believes in working with the community. He is a dynamic motivational speaker, workshop facilitator and has trained as a Mentor and Life Coach. He has worked under acclaimed Los Angeles gang mediator Twilight Bey as a Youth Engagement Practitioner in the inner cities of London. He specializes in personal development, leadership and has been accredited to deliver the A-mer-i-Can curriculum (known as My-I-Can in the U.K) and Bob Proctor's *Life Success*